A Visit to
GREECE

Peter & Connie Roop

Heinemann Library
Des Plaines, Illinois

Designed by AMR
Illustrations by Art Construction
Printed in Hong Kong / China

02 01 00
10 9 8 7 6 5 4 3 2

Library of Congress Cataloging-in-Publication Data

Roop, Peter.
    Greece / Peter & Connie Roop.
        p.   cm. -- (A visit to)
    K-2.
    Summary: Introduces the country of Greece, including the land, landmarks, homes, food, clothes, work, transportation, language, school, sports, celebrations, and the arts.
    ISBN 1-57572-709-9 (library binding)
    1. Greece--Juvenile literature.   [1. Greece.] I. Roop, Connie.
II. Title. III. Series: Roop, Peter. Visit to.
DF717.R66   1998
949.5--DC21
                                                    98-12450
                                                    AC

Acknowledgments
The Publishers would like to thank the following for permission to reproduce photographs:
J. Allan Cash: pp. 6, 7, 8, 9, 10, 11, 18, 19, 21, 28; Hutchison Library: J. Egan p. p5, 16, R. Giling pp. 12, 23, 25, 29, S. Molins p. 14, I. Tree p. 13; Travel Ink: I. Booth p. 17, N. Bowen-Morris p. 26, A. Lewis p. 24; Trip: B. North p. 15, H. Rogers p. 20, V. Sidoropolev p. 27, A. Tovy p. 22

Cover photograph reproduced with permission of J. Hartley, Panos Pictures

Every effort has been made to contact copyright holders of any material reproduced in this book. Any omissions will be rectified in subsequent printings if notice is given to the Publisher.

Any words appearing in bold, **like this,** are explained in the Glossary.

Contents

Greece

Key
- Land above 3,300 ft/1000 m
- Land above 0 ft/m/sea level
- ● Capital
- ● Important cities

Salonica

▲ Mt. Olympus
9,626 ft/2917 m

North

G R E E C E

Athens

MEDITERRANEAN SEA

Greece is in **Europe**. Most of the **mainland** is surrounded by the Mediterranean Sea. Greece has about 2,000 islands of all sizes. People live on 160 of the islands.

Many people visit Greece to go to its beautiful beaches. Greeks eat, sleep, play, and go to school like you. Life in Greece is also **unique**.

Land

Mountains cover most of Greece.
The biggest ones are in the middle of
Greece. There are a few small rivers,
but these dry up in the hot summer.

Most of the lowland is next to the sea. Many towns and cities are on these lowlands.

Landmarks

Mount Olympus is the highest mountain in Greece. Long ago, the Greeks believed that gods lived on the top of Mount Olympus.

Greece has many **ancient** buildings. The Parthenon is one of the most famous. It was built almost 2,500 years ago as a **temple** for Athena, the goddess of Athens.

Homes

The two biggest cities in Greece are Athens and Salonica. One out of three Greeks live in or near Athens. Families live in small apartments because the city is so crowded.

Most Greeks live in the country. Their homes usually have four or five rooms, flat roofs, and white walls. Some Greeks grow plants up the walls for the fruit and for decoration.

Food

The Greeks eat **seafood** from the Mediterranean Sea. The main meat eaten is lamb. Olive oil is used in much of the cooking.

Lunch is the main meal of the day.
The whole family eats together.
People often take an afternoon nap,
away from the heat of the day.

Clothes

Most Greeks wear clothes like yours.
Some older Greeks wear black when
they go out. They do this to show **respect**
for family members who have died.

The Greeks' **national** dress is a white
shirt, a red hat, and a white skirt.
Men, women, and children wear this
for special celebrations and dances.

Work

Many Greeks are farmers. They grow wheat, tobacco, cotton, grapes, and olives. They also keep sheep and goats for their milk. The milk is made into yogurt and cheese.

Many Greeks work with **tourists**. They help the people who visit Greece every year. They work in hotels, restaurants, shops, and transportation.

Transportation

People travel by **old-fashioned** and **modern** transportation. In the country, many villages only have dirt roads so donkeys are a good way of carrying heavy loads.

Greek shipping companies are famous around the world. Ships also carry **tourists** between Greek islands or take them on cruises around the Mediterranean Sea.

Language

Most Greeks speak the Greek language.
Greek is the oldest language spoken in
Europe. Many Greeks also speak English.

Greek has its own alphabet of 24 letters. Many signs are written in both the Greek and **Roman** alphabets.

School

Greek children go to school from ages six to fifteen. They learn math, art, music, religion, history, and physical education.

Greek is the main language taught in
school. Many children learn English or
French, too.

Free Time

The Olympic Games were first held in Greece over 2,000 years ago. Today, almost all Greeks enjoy soccer and swimming.

The evening walk is a time for family and friends to visit. Adults also go to coffeehouses to play cards and meet with their friends.

Celebrations

Easter is the most important festival in
Greece. The Greeks celebrate other **religious**
festivals, too. Priests wear special robes and
lead parades through the streets.

At some festivals, the Greeks dress up in **traditional** costumes and celebrate with dancing and singing.

The Arts

People have written and **performed** plays in Greece for over 2,000 years. Today, both old and new plays are performed in the **ancient** theaters.

The *bouzouki* is a Greek string instrument.
Musicians play **traditional** songs on the
bouzouki. The songs are happy and sad.

Fact File

Name	The full name of Greece is the Hellenic Republic.
Capital	The **capital** city of Greece is Athens.
Languages	Most Greeks speak Greek and many can also speak English.
Population	There are about 10½ million people living in Greece.
Money	Instead of the dollar, the Greeks have the *drachma* (drahk-mah).
Religion	Most Greeks believe in Greek Orthodoxy, which is part of the Christian church.
Products	Greece produces lots of olives and olive oil, cotton, grapes, tobacco, oil, and some metals.

Words You Can Learn

enas (eh-nah)	one
dhio (theeoh)	two
tris (treace)	three
ya sis (yah soos)	hello
andio (a-DEoh)	goodbye
efharisto (efkha-REE stoh)	thank you
parakalo (barata-LOH)	please
ne (neh)	yes
ohi (okhi)	no

Glossary

ancient	from a long time ago
capital	the city where the government is based
Europe	a group of countries north of the Mediterranean Sea
mainland	a country's largest part that is land
modern	new and up-to-date
national	shared by a nation or country
old-fashioned	from the past
performed	acted out on stage
religious	to do with people's beliefs
respect	to think highly of someone
Roman	the letters that you read and write that make up English
seafood	fish and shellfish
temple	a building used as a place of worship
tourist	a person traveling on vacation
traditional	the way something has been done or made for a very long time
unique	different in a special way

Index

More Books to Read

Allard, Denise. *Greece*. Chatham, NJ: Raintree Steck-Vaughn. 1997.

Jacobsen, Karen. *Greece*. Danbury, CT: Children's Press. 1990.